C'est l'automne

C'est l'automne

Jimmy Pickering

Texte français de Caroline Ricard

À Leota

(Mère Nature dans une limousine)

Merci de m'avoir fait découvrir que chaque nouvelle saison
est un cadeau extraordinaire

Suzie et Sam découvrent, par la fenêtre,
qu'un vent froid siffle entre les branches du grand hêtre.

Les feuilles qui étaient vertes
se sont colorées

de teintes jaunes,
rouges et orangées.

La nouvelle saison est arrivée;
et Sam et Suzie vont partager
tous les petits plaisirs
que l'automne peut offrir.

Des feuilles tombées sont mises dans des sacs;
les autres sont tranformées en montagnes et en lacs.

Suzie et Sam sautent sur le sol,
puis bondissent vers les cieux,

et s'amusent de voir
toutes les feuilles collées sur eux.

Puis vient la tarte à la citrouille,
ce succulent dessert d'automne,
qui calme les gargouillements
des gloutons et des gloutonnes.

Pour Suzie et Sam,
ce délice est meilleur accompagné
de sucre, de cannelle
et d'une montagne de crème fouettée.

Un cheval et une charrette

pour une promenade à deux,

juste Suzie et Sam

dans un paysage merveilleux.

La visite au verger
se déroule dans la gaieté.
Ils cueillent des fruits rougeoyants
sous le soleil éclatant!

Il y a tellement de pommes
qu'ils n'arrêtent d'en ramasser
que lorsque leurs paniers
sont remplis à craquer.

La vieille foire du comté
est de retour chaque année.

Avec ses jeux, manèges et sucreries,

elle ravit grands et petits.

La foire offre à tous de nombreuses activités.

Ils choisissent la petite ferme pour commencer.

Suzie nourrit les poussins duveteux.

Sam, quant à lui, doit surveiller sa queue.

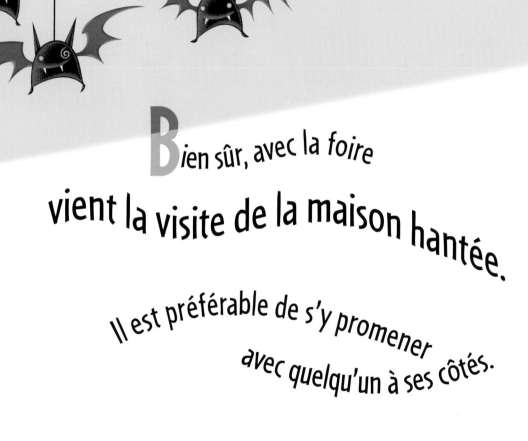

Bien sûr, avec la foire

vient la visite de la maison hantée.

Il est préférable de s'y promener
avec quelqu'un à ses côtés.

L'automne est la saison rêvée
pour transformer une citrouille
en œuvre d'art.

Suzie et Sam, bien sûr,
ne manqueront pas
de faire leur part.

Leurs citrouilles sont terminées.
Les lumières sont tamisées
pour le plaisir de s'effrayer.
L'Halloween pourra bientôt débuter.

Mais il leur faut trouver des costumes
qui feront très peur!
Suzie se transforme en mort-vivant
pour cette nuit de l'horreur.

Sam, lui, est déguisé en poulpe géant.
Avec ses bras impressionnants,
il est prêt à effrayer
tous les gens du quartier.

Attraper des pommes avec les dents
est un jeu très amusant!

Pour réussir, il faut bien viser
les beaux fruits rouges convoités.

Après avoir bien rigolé,
ils sont prêts à rentrer.

Sam rit de Suzie
qui est mouillée de la tête aux pieds.

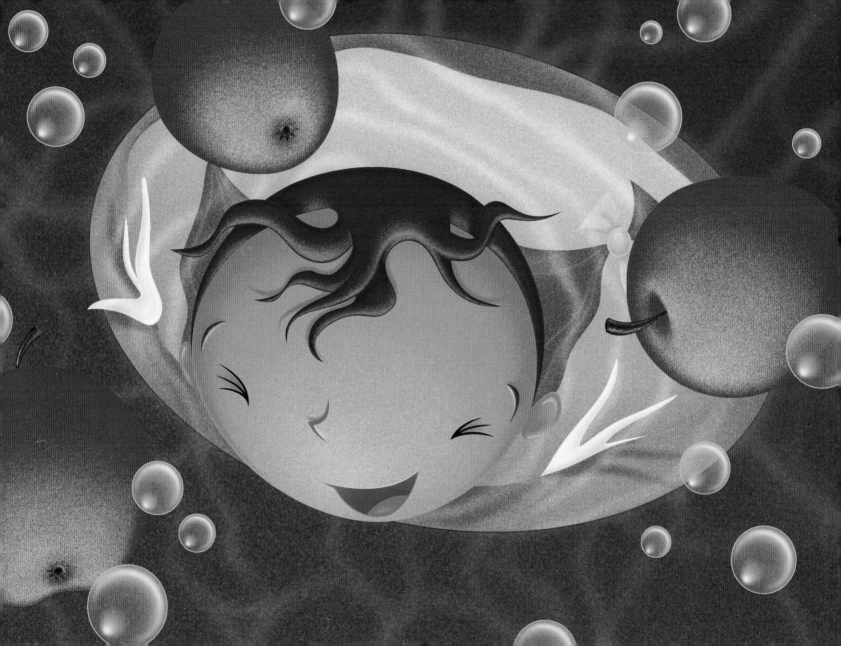

Rien de mieux qu'un cidre chaud

pour chasser tous les frissons;

un jour d'automne où il fait froid,

miam, que c'est bon!

En cette première nuit d'automne,
au lit, chaudement emmitouflés,

les amis constatent que cette journée

les a **vraiment épuisés.**

Mais fatigués ou non,
ils sont heureux de repenser

au plaisir et **aux frissons**

que l'automne peut leur donner.

Catalogage avant publication de Bibliothèque et Archives Canada

Pickering, Jimmy

C'est l'automne / Jimmy Pickering; texte français de Caroline Ricard.

Traduction de : It's Fall.

Pour les 4-8 ans.

ISBN 0-439-94851-7

I. Ricard, Caroline, 1978- II. Titre.

PZ23.P5525Cea 2005   j813'.6   C2005-903098-4

Édition publiée par les Éditions Scholastic, 175 Hillmount Road, Markham (Ontario) L6C 1Z7, avec la permission de Tallfellow Press, Inc.

5 4 3 2 1   Imprimé au Canada   05 06 07 08

THE INCREDIBLE WORK OF ENGINEERS

WITH MAX AXIOM SUPER SCIENTIST

by Agnieszka Biskup

illustrated by Marcelo Baez

Consultant:
Morgan Hynes, PhD
Research Assistant Professor, Education
Research Program Manager
Center for Engineering Education and Outreach
Tufts University
Medford, Massachusetts

CAPSTONE PRESS
a capstone imprint

Library of Congress Cataloging-in-Publication Data
Biskup, Agnieszka.
  The incredible work of engineers with Max Axiom, super scientist / by Agnieszka
Biskup ; illustrated by Marcelo Baez.
      p. cm.—(Graphic library. Graphic science and engineering in action)
  Includes bibliographical references and index.
  ISBN 978-1-4296-9937-2 (library binding)
  ISBN 978-1-62065-705-8 (paperback)
  ISBN 978-1-4765-1591-5 (ebook PDF)
  1. Engineering—Comic books, strips, etc.—Juvenile literature. 2. Graphic novels. I.
Baez, Marcelo, illustrator. II. Title.
  TA149.B57 2013
  620.0023—dc23   2012026439

Summary: In graphic novel format, follows the adventures of Max Axiom as he learns
about what engineers do and how they work.

Designer
Ted Williams

Media Researcher
Wanda Winch

Production Specialist
Laura Manthe

Editor
Christopher L. Harbo

Printed in the United States of America in Brainerd, Minnesota.
092012   006938BANGS13

TABLE of CONTENTS

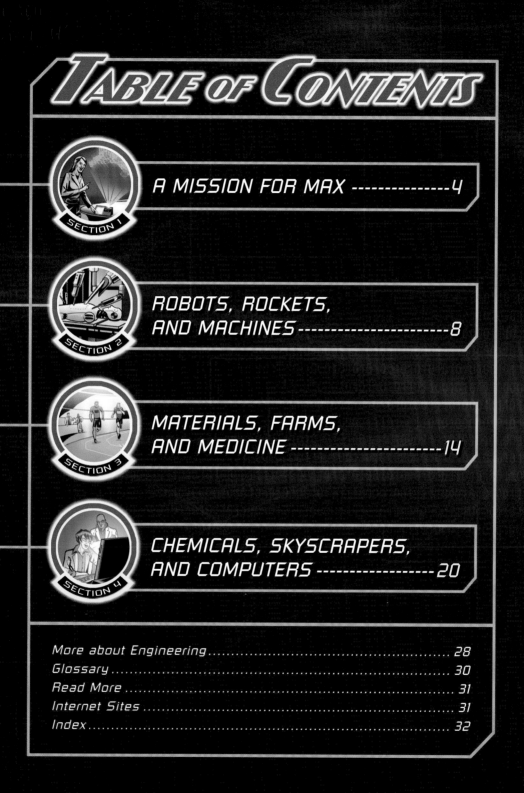

The Federal Space Exploration Agency wants to build a colony on the moon. This base will give scientists a place to live while they study the moon.

Building a lunar colony will take an outstanding team of engineers. We want you to interview and report back on the best engineers for the job.

I know I can find engineers who are up for the task.

I look forward to meeting them.

I've got some engineers in mind, and I've sent them messages to let them know I'm coming. Now I just need to see them in action.

Engineers build airplanes that stay in the sky and skyscrapers that don't fall down.

Engineers also solve challenging problems to help make the world a better place to live.

They look for ways to design engines that use less fuel. They create materials that can withstand fires. They develop safer roads.

VVROOM!!

They make sure that the things we use are safe and work properly.

A lunar colony needs many different things for people to live there, stay healthy, and be safe.

To design and build it, we're going to need a lot of different engineers.

Scientist vs. Engineer
Scientists and engineers are not the same thing. An engineer once said scientists discover the world that exists and engineers create the world that never was. But scientists and engineers often work together. Engineers use science to build things that haven't existed before. And scientists need engineers to design and build the instruments and tools they use to make their discoveries.

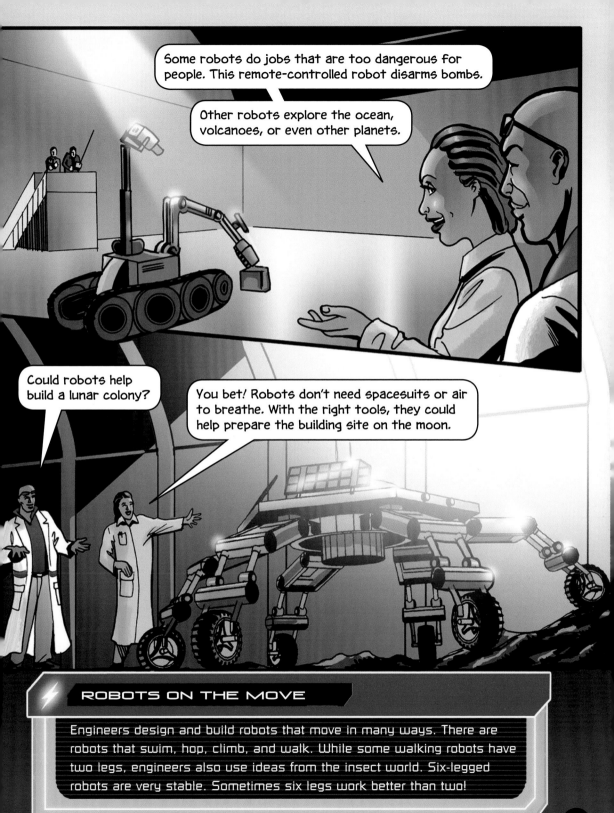

Some robots do jobs that are too dangerous for people. This remote-controlled robot disarms bombs.

Other robots explore the ocean, volcanoes, or even other planets.

Could robots help build a lunar colony?

You bet! Robots don't need spacesuits or air to breathe. With the right tools, they could help prepare the building site on the moon.

ROBOTS ON THE MOVE

Engineers design and build robots that move in many ways. There are robots that swim, hop, climb, and walk. While some walking robots have two legs, engineers also use ideas from the insect world. Six-legged robots are very stable. Sometimes six legs work better than two!

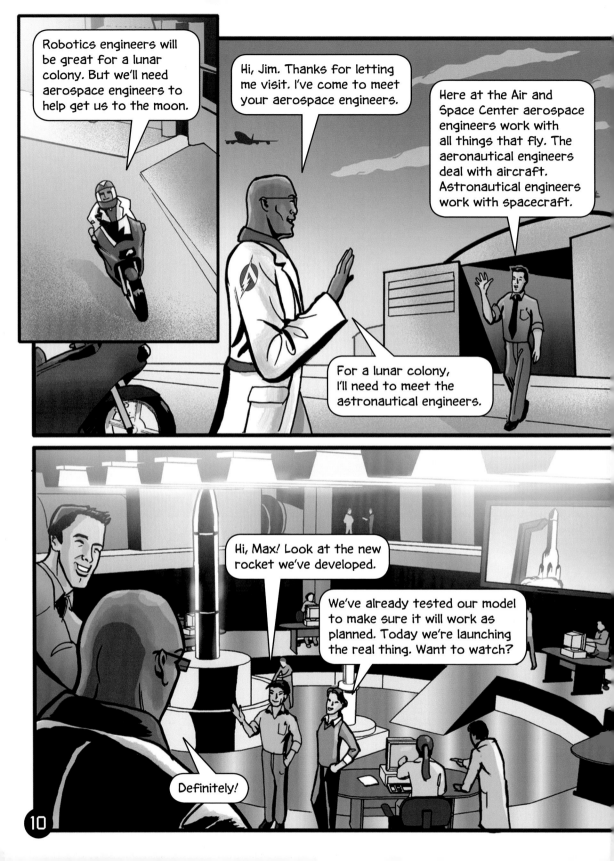

Teamwork in engineering is important because we need the knowledge of many people to build a complex machine.
For instance, I designed the rocket's structure so it can travel at high speeds.
I engineered the navigation system so the rocket goes where we want it to go.
And I built the rocket boosters that make it fly.
The launch is a success!
RROOAARR!
Maybe this type of rocket will take us to the moon again.
Thanks for showing me around, Jim. Now I'm meeting with one of your mechanical engineers.
You must mean Ann. She's working at the wind tunnel.

Hi, Max! Let me show you what's going on in the materials engineering lab.

Thanks, John.

Everything we see, use, and touch is made of materials.

Some materials, such as wood, are natural. But others, such as plastic, are created in a lab. As a materials engineer, I pick the right material for the product.

Picking the right material is really important for how things work. You wouldn't want a running shoe made out of wood.

I also develop and test new materials used to create anything from this running shoe to spacecraft.

It sounds like materials engineers help create materials to make things work better.

That's right. I design new materials to have certain properties depending on what they're used for.

I'm developing a metal that's lighter and stronger than steel for military trucks. Lighter trucks would move faster and easier on the battlefield.

What kind of materials would you create for working on the moon?

Hmm. A material for spacecraft and spacesuits that could self-heal cracks might be useful to keep astronauts safe.

That would be an awesome material for a lunar colony. Thanks for your time, John.

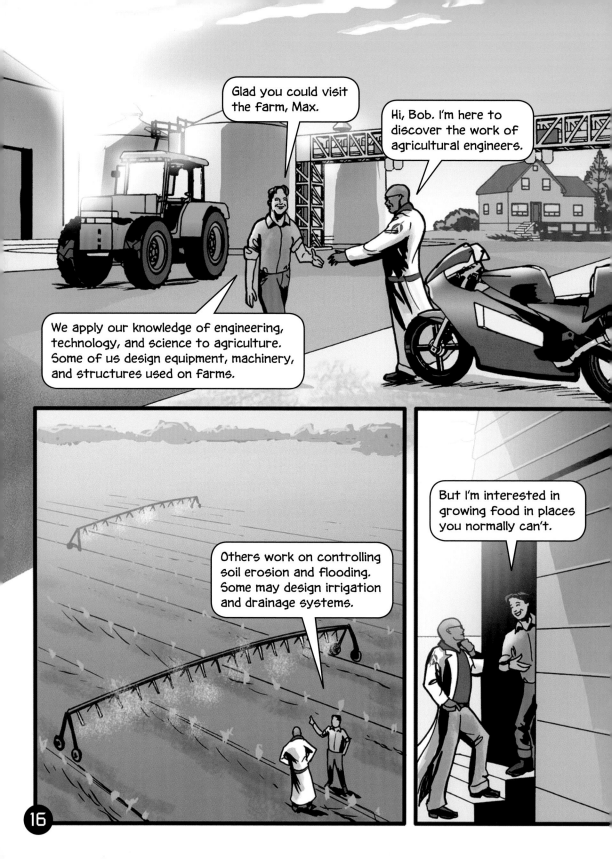

My growth chamber is a climate-controlled environment that feeds plants automatically. It grows fruits and vegetables year-round and in the harshest environments.
Feeding our lunar colonists will be very important.
Would your growth chamber work on the moon?
It's worked at the South Pole. I think it could be adapted to grow plants in the moon's lower gravity.
It's good to see that engineers don't just work with machines. Speaking of which, my next stop is to see how bioengineers apply engineering principles to biology and medicine.
Have fun, Max!

We've even built artificial sprinting feet like these blades. They allow disabled athletes to compete against people without disabilities.

How would bioengineering help in a lunar colony?

Bioengineers could develop medical sensors to monitor a person's health. Placed under the skin, these sensors will make sure colonists are doing well during the mission.

Good point. Our colonists will need the same medical attention on the moon as they would on Earth. Thanks, Lee!

Seeing Inside the Body

Bioengineers also design scanning systems for the human body. A CT scanner is a special X-ray machine. It takes hundreds of pictures to create a 3D image of a person's body. Doctors use CT scans to help diagnose disease.

CHEMICALS, SKYSCRAPERS, AND COMPUTERS

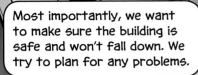

Most importantly, we want to make sure the building is safe and won't fall down. We try to plan for any problems.

Like what?

This building must withstand strong storms, floods, and earthquakes. We follow standards and building codes to keep buildings safe.

Our lunar colony may have moonquakes. What kinds of habitats could we build?

The buildings will need to bend and shake without cracking and leaking air. A civil engineer can help you develop solutions.

Excellent! We'll look forward to your help.

ENGINEERING

 Many astronauts are engineers. Neil Armstrong, the first man to walk on the moon, had a degree in aeronautical engineering. Buzz Aldrin, the second man to walk on the moon, was a mechanical engineer.

Materials engineers study how long a metal part can last in a machine or structure. Metal parts can fail due to temperature and stress. A part failure can be deadly if it happens in an airplane engine or a bridge. You can see how stress makes metal fail by bending a paper clip back and forth in the same spot. Eventually it will snap in two.

Chemical engineers improve medications. They find better ways to produce large amounts of new vaccines. They also figure out how to store medicines longer and how to develop drugs with fewer side effects.

The pyramids in Egypt are some of the earliest examples of large-scale engineering. The ancient Egyptian Imhotep designed and built the first pyramid for King Djoser more than 4,000 years ago. Imhotep was one of the world's first engineers. He's also the first one we know by name.

 In ancient Rome, civil engineers created large public works. More than 2,000 years ago, Roman engineers built aqueducts. These channels carried clean water into the city. They also built a system of roads to link the cities in their empire.

When people think about engineering wonders, big things come to mind. Civil engineers built the Golden Gate Bridge, the Panama Canal, and the Hoover Dam. They also built the tallest building in the world, Dubai's Burj Khalifa. It stands 2,723 feet (830 meters) tall.

The National Academy of Engineering listed the greatest engineering achievements of the 20th century that have changed our lives. Use of electricity was number one, followed by the car and the airplane. The Internet was number 13.

MORE ABOUT

MAX AXIOM
SUPER SCIENTIST

Real name: Maxwell J. Axiom
Hometown: Seattle, Washington
Height: 6' 1"   Weight: 192 lbs
Eyes: Brown   Hair: None

Super capabilities: Super intelligence; able to shrink to the size of an atom; sunglasses give x-ray vision; lab coat allows for travel through time and space.

Origin: Since birth, Max Axiom seemed destined for greatness. His mother, a marine biologist, taught her son about the mysteries of the sea. His father, a nuclear physicist and volunteer park ranger, schooled Max on the wonders of earth and sky.

One day on a wilderness hike, a megacharged lightning bolt struck Max with blinding fury. When he awoke, Max discovered a newfound energy and set out to learn as much about science as possible. He traveled the globe earning degrees in every aspect of the field. Upon his return, he was ready to share his knowledge and new identity with the world. He had become Max Axiom, Super Scientist.

Glossary

aeronautical (ayr-oh-NAW-tuh-kuhl)—having to do with designing and building aircraft

aerospace (AYR-oh-spays)—having to do with designing and building aircraft and spacecraft

artificial (ar-tuh-FI-shuhl)—made by people

astronautical (ass-truh-NAW-ti-kuhl)—having to do with designing and building spacecraft

biology (bye-OL-uh-jee)—the study of plant and animal life

colony (KAH-luh-nee)—a place that is settled by a group of people who live together in the same area

diagnose (dy-ig-NOHS)—to find the cause of a problem

environment (en-VYE-ruhn-muhnt)—the natural world of the land, water, and air

erosion (i-ROH-zhuhn)—the wearing away of land by water or wind

irrigation (ihr-uh-GAY-shuhn)—supplying water to crops using a system of pipes or channels

lunar (LOO-nur)—having to do with a moon

navigation (NAV-uh-gay-shun)—the science of plotting and following a course from one place to another

property (PROP-ur-tee)—quality in a material, such as color, hardness, or shape

technology (tek-NOL-uh-jee)—the use of science to do practical things, such as designing complex machines

vaccine (vak-SEEN)—a medicine that prevents a disease

READ MORE

Enz, Tammy. *Zoom It: Invent New Machines that Move.* Invent It. Mankato, Minn. Capstone Press, 2012.

Graham, Ian. *Massive Monsters and Other Huge Megastructures.* Megastructures. Mankato, Minn.: QEB Pub., 2012.

Gray, Susan Heinrichs. *Bioengineer.* Cool Science Careers. Ann Arbor, Mich.: Cherry Lake Pub., 2011.

Solway, Andrew. *Buildings and Structures.* Science and Technology. Chicago: Raintree, 2011.

INTERNET SITES

FactHound offers a safe, fun way to find Internet sites related to this book. All sites on FactHound have been researched by our staff.

Here's all you do:

Visit *www.facthound.com*

Type in this code: 9781429699372

Check out projects, games and lots more at
www.capstonekids.com

INDEX